MOTOCROSS
TURNS AND BERMS

BY LISA J. AMSTUTZ

CAPSTONE PRESS
a capstone imprint

Published by Capstone Press, an imprint of Capstone
1710 Roe Crest Drive, North Mankato, Minnesota 56003
capstonepub.com

Copyright © 2026 by Capstone. All rights reserved. No part of this publication may be reproduced in whole or in part, or stored in a retrieval system, or transmitted in any form or by any means, electronic, mechanical, photocopying, recording, or otherwise, without written permission of the publisher.

Library of Congress Cataloging-in-Publication Data
Names: Amstutz, Lisa J., author.
Title: Motocross : turns and berms / by Lisa J. Amstutz.
Description: North Mankato, Minnesota : Capstone Press, [2026] | Series: Dirt bike blast | Includes bibliographical references and index. | Audience: Ages 9-11 | Audience: Grades 4-6 | Summary: "Motocross riders roar over whoops, sail over jumps, and speed up and down hills. They have one goal—to claim victory when the checkered flag waves. Freestyle motocross riders perform daring, high-flying tricks to earn the top prize. Put readers in the center of the heart-pumping motocross action as they learn about everything from rules to equipment and track features. Carefully leveled, high-energy text helps ensure accessibility for even the most reluctant readers"— Provided by publisher.
Identifiers: LCCN 2024054348 (print) | LCCN 2024054349 (ebook) | ISBN 9798875226090 (hardcover) | ISBN 9798875226045 (paperback) | ISBN 9798875226052 (pdf) | ISBN 9798875226069 (epub) | ISBN 9798875226076 (kindle edition)
Subjects: LCSH: Motocross—Juvenile literature.
Classification: LCC GV1060.12 .A47 2026 (print) | LCC GV1060.12 (ebook) | DDC 796.7/56—dc23/eng/20250110
LC record available at https://lccn.loc.gov/2024054348
LC ebook record available at https://lccn.loc.gov/2024054349

Editorial Credits
Editor: Carrie Sheely; Designer: Dina Her; Media Researcher: Rebekah Hubstenberger; Production Specialist: Tori Abraham

Image Credits
Alamy: Belga News Agency, 16, Cal Sport Media, 26, Gordon Allison, 12, Heritage Image Partnership Ltd, 18, Nderim Kaceli, 17, Thurman James/Cal Sport Media, 13, 14, Tony Watson, 19; Associated Press: James Quigg/The Daily Press, 24, Mark J. Terrill, 29; Getty Images: Alex Grimm/Bongarts, 27, Cameron Smith, 25, Dean Mouhtaropoulos, 7, Harry How, 28, Sebastian Marko/Red Bull, 21, Thananuwat Srirasant, 23; Shutterstock: CTR Photos, 8, Gints Ivuskans, 11, sainthorant, cover, Stephen Coburn, 22, StockStudio Aerials, 15, Suvorov_Alex, 4-5, Yurchenko S, 20, YuryKo, 10

Design Elements
Shutterstock: backup, Goromaru, JACKREZNOR, Miloje, salam kerrong

Any additional websites and resources referenced in this book are not maintained, authorized, or sponsored by Capstone. All product and company names are trademarks™ or registered® trademarks of their respective holders.

TABLE OF CONTENTS

All About Motocross Racing 6

Race Time 12

Wheels Up! 18

Fierce Competition 24

    Glossary 30

    Read More 31

    Internet Sites 31

    Index 32

    About the Author 32

Words in **bold** are in the glossary.

WHAT IS MOTOCROSS?

Motocross races take place on an outdoor dirt track. Riders sail over jumps and around tight turns. In freestyle motocross, riders do not race. They go over big jumps and do tricks in midair. Judges score the tricks.

knobby tires

stiff suspension

CHAPTER 1
ALL ABOUT MOTOCROSS RACING

High-flying jumps. Blistering speed. Twists and turns. What motorsport includes all of these? Motocross!

Each motocross event has two races. They are called **motos**. Riders earn points for each one. First place gets the most points. Last place gets the least. The two scores are added. The person with the most points wins!

FACT

The first official motocross race was held in 1924 in the United Kingdom. The races came to the U.S. in the 1960s.

berm

Rumble! Machines pack dirt to make a racetrack. It will be 1 to 3 miles (1.6 to 4.8 kilometers) long. There are turns, jumps, and hills. Some turns have **berms** at the edge. No two courses are the same.

FACT

Motocross racers compete in different classes. Some are based on a bike's engine. There may be classes for bikes with 250-cc and 450-cc engines.

Time to suit up! Racing can be dangerous. Many crashes happen. Riders need safety gear. They wear a helmet, goggles, boots, and gloves. They wear pants and long-sleeved shirts. Riders wear chest protectors. Some clothing has built-in padding.

CHAPTER 2
RACE TIME

The racers line up. Engines rev. The gates drop. And they're off! Who will get the **hole shot**? This rider leads at the first turn.

The gates drop to start a race.

The racers lean into tight corners. They slide through mud. They speed over rows of small bumps called whoops.

Riders fight to get the hole shot.

Here come the jumps! These can be as high as 20 feet (6 meters). There may be several jumps in a row. Two jumps are called a double. Three jumps are a triple.

Watch out! Next up is a tabletop!

It is a flat, raised jump.

FACT

Tracks might have step-ups and step-downs. Step-ups are jumps that lead to a higher landing area. Step-downs lead to a lower landing area.

It's the last lap. The checkered flag waves. The racers stop at the **pits**. They check their bikes. They get ready for the next moto.

Soon they're off again! They do another moto. Then the scores are added. The winners celebrate on the **podium**.

Winners of a women's motocross race in Italy

CHAPTER 3
WHEELS UP!

Flip! Twist! Turn! Freestyle motocross (FMX) riders show off their amazing tricks. This kind of motocross is not a race. Riders are scored on their skills.

Hart attack

An FMX rider starts a **routine**. First up is the Hart attack. He holds onto the bike seat. His feet fly above his head. Wow!

FACT
The Hart attack is named for the rider who invented it, Carey Hart.

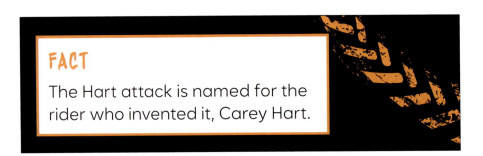

Another rider does a rock solid. He lets go with both hands. He follows this trick with a whip. The bike turns sideways in the air. The crowd cheers.

Rock solid

The crowd looks up in awe. A rider is doing a cliffhanger! The rider's feet are under the handlebars. Nothing else is holding onto the bike!

Cliffhanger

The next rider pushes his body into the air. His feet trail behind him. He looks like he is flying! What is the name of this amazing trick? The Superman!

CHAPTER 4
FIERCE COMPETITION

Motocross events are fun to watch. There may be one near you! **Amateurs** and professionals compete. There are races for kids. Some start at age 4.

Pros compete in several events and series. One is the American Motorcyclist Association (AMA) Pro Motocross Championship series. Another is the Motocross World Championship series. Top FMX riders compete at the X Games.

Dylan Ferrandis competes in an AMA Pro Motocross Championship event in California.

Josh Sheehan competes at the X Games.

Many pros have led the way in motocross. Ashley Fiolek started racing at age 7. She won four AMA Women's Pro Motocross Championships. Ricky Carmichael is a motocross racing legend. He won more than 100 races.

Ashley Fiolek celebrates after a win.

Travis Pastrana performs the first double backflip in competition.

In 2006, Travis Pastrana became the first rider to land a double backflip in competition. He has won several X Games gold medals in FMX. Who will the next legend be?

GLOSSARY

amateur (AM-uh-chur)—an athlete who takes part in a sport for pleasure rather than for money

berm (BURM)—a banked turn or corner on a racetrack

hole shot (HOL SHOT)—when a racer leads around the first turn of a motocross race

moto (MOH-toh)—a single motocross race; each event includes two motos

pit (PIT)—a place where racers can add fuel or make repairs to their vehicles

podium (POH-dee-uhm)—a platform where winners receive their prizes

routine (roo-TEEN)—a planned set of moves in a performance or contest

READ MORE

Abdo, Kenny. *Motocross*. Minneapolis: Abdo Zoom, 2024.

Conaghan, Bernard. *Motocross*. New York: Crabtree Publishing, 2023.

Golusky, Jackie. *Motocross: Rev It Up!* Minneapolis: Lerner Publications, 2023.

INTERNET SITES

American Motorcyclist Association: Motocross
americanmotorcyclist.com/racing/motocross

Kiddle: Motocross Facts for Kids
kids.kiddle.co/Motocross

X Games
xgames.com

INDEX

Carmichael, Ricky, 28
classes, 9
cliffhanger, 22

double backflips, 29

engines, 9, 12

Fiolek, Ashley, 28

Hart attack, 20

jumps, 4, 6, 9, 14, 15

Pastrana, Travis, 29
podiums, 17
points, 6
Pro Motocross
  Championship series,
  26, 28

rock solid, 21

safety gear, 10
Superman, 23

whips, 21
whoops, 13
World Championship
  series, 26

X Games, 26, 27, 29

ABOUT THE AUTHOR

Lisa J. Amstutz is the author of more than 150 children's books on topics ranging from applesauce to zebra mussels. An ecologist by training, she enjoys sharing her love of nature with kids. Lisa lives on a small farm with her family.